Alice in Wonderland

A Page to Panto script
by
Joe Meloy

Alice in Wonderland
A pantomime in 2 acts

First Published in Great Britain in 2023 by Beercott Books.

Copyright: © Joe Meloy 2023

ISBN:978-1-7393020-1-6

www.beercottbooks.co.uk

Beercott

For my **Dad**,

reckon...

MAIN CHARACTERS

ALICE - The girl who falls through the rabbit whole into Wonderland

DUCHESS DOLLY DOLLOP - The Dame. Mother of Wally.

WALLY THE WHITE RABBIT - The Comic. Son of Duchess Dolly Dollop and always running late

QUEEN OF HEARTS - The Villain. A woman who is obsessed with jam tarts and chopping off people's heads.

KING OF HEARTS - The Villain's loving husband

KNAVE OF HEARTS - The unfortunate Jack of Hearts who is put on trial for a crime he didn't commit.

MAD HATTER - Mad as a box of frogs, loves to throw an unbirthday tea party.

DORMOUSE - An attendee at the Unbirthday tea party

MARCH HARE - An attendee at the Unbirthday tea party

CATERPILLAR - A mellowed out little worm

CHESHIRE CAT - The coolest cat in Wonderland

DODO - A singer at the Wonderland Show Bar

DUCK - A singer at the Wonderland Show Bar

TWEEDLE DEE - An odd fellow. The twin of Tweedle Dum.

TWEEDLE DUM - An odd fellow. The twin of Tweedle Dee.

SMALL SPEAKING ROLES

CARD GUARDS -
  Two of Diamonds
  Three of Diamonds
  Ace of Diamonds
  Seven of Spades
  Eight of Spades
  Two of Clubs
  Four of Clubs
  Five of Clubs
  Two of Hearts
  Nine of Hearts

ENSEMBLE - Various Creatures, a Ghost and Card Guards

<h1 style="text-align:center">SCENES</h1>

ACT 1

PROLOGUE - Front of tabs

SCENE 1 - Wonderland Forest

SCENE 2 - The Caterpillar's Leaf

SCENE 3 - Tweedle Dee and Tweedle Dum's Cottage

SCENE 4 - Wonderland Show Bar

SCENE 5 - Queen of Hart's Castle

SCENE 6 - The Mad Hatter's House

ACT 2

SCENE 1 - Queen of Hart's Castle

SCENE 2 - Wonderland Forest

SCENE 3 - Queen of Hart's Castle

SCENE 4 - The Duchess's Cottage

SCENE 5 - Queen of Hart's Castle

SCENE 6 - In front of tabs

SCENE 7 - Bows.

PROLOGUE

IN FRONT OF TABS

(The show opens with the noise of several alarm clocks sounding. The sound grows until eventually WALLY THE WHITE RABBIT runs down from the back of the auditorium.)

WALLY: *(Whilst running down towards the stage)* I'm late! I'm late! I'm very, very late! *(When he gets to the stage, he takes out his pocket watch)* Goodness me I'm so incredibly late! *(Notices the audience)*. Oh, hang on a second, I might be late but I didn't notice all of you! Why didn't any of you tell me I was late? I'm going to be in such trouble with the Duchess! Duchess Dolly of Wonderland that is! Don't worry you'll meet her a bit later on I'm sure… Just a minute I haven't even introduced myself!

I'm the White Rabbit, but you can call me Wally! And I live in Wonderland, and I need your help as I'm always late so every time I run on I'm going to shout 'What time is it?' And you need to shout, 'you're late!' That way at least I know I'm late! Let's give that a go! What time is it? *(Audience: You're late!)* I'm sure you can do it better than that! What time is it? *(Audience: You're late!)* And once more for luck! What time is it? *(Audience: You're late!)* Brilliant thanks everyone!

Now I'm just about to take a trip down the rabbit hole, which is the entrance to Wonderland! Would you like to join me in Wonderland? *(audience response)* I said would you like to come to Wonderland with me? *(audience response)* Well, you'll have to be a little bit louder than that!

Would you like to come with me? *(audience response)* That's much better! What's wonderland like I hear you ask? Well it's like… It's like… Well why don't I show you!

(The curtains open to reveal Wonderland in full swing there are several weird and wonderful characters a mixture of birds, playing cards, and other mythical creatures, the stage is full of vibrant colour)

Song 1 – WALLY & CAST

(Blackout)

SCENE ONE

WONDERLAND FOREST

(ALICE runs on from the back of the auditorium)

ALICE: White Rabbit! White Rabbit! Wait for me! *(Once on the stage ALICE has a look around)* My what a strange place! This is like no place I've been before! I wish I could find that White Rabbit! *(To the audience)* Have any of you seen him? *(WALLY runs behind ALICE and hides)* Where is he? *(Audience: he's behind you!)* Where? *(Audience: behind you!)* I can't see him anywhere!

(WALLY jumps out from his hiding place)

WALLY: What time is it? *(Audience: You're late!)* I say Mary-Ann where have you been?

ALICE: But-

WALLY: None of this Mary-Ann I need you to go and fetch my silk gloves!

ALICE: But I'm-

WALLY: What are you doing still standing there Mary-Ann?

ALICE: I'm not Mary-Ann!

WALLY: But you look so much like my servant girl Mary-Ann! Are you sure you're not her?

ALICE: Quite sure yes!

WALLY: Only quite sure?

ALICE: I'm entirely sure I'm not Mary-Ann. My name is Alice.

WALLY: Well lovely to meet you Alice, I'm the White Rabbit, but you can call me Wally!

ALICE: Well, it's a pleasure to meet you, Wally!

WALLY: *(Has a sudden moment of realisation)* Hang on a minute! How did you get into Wonderland?

ALICE: Easy I followed you down the rabbit hole.

WALLY: Well, that makes sense, *(pointing at the audience)*, but what about all this lot out here?

ALICE: I think they paid to get in.

WALLY: Who would pay to get in here!

DUCHESS: *(From offstage)* Wally!

WALLY: That's my Mum the Duchess! If she finds out I've been late again, she'll go mad! Quick follow me!

(Exit ALICE and WALLY. Enter DUCHESS)

DUCHESS: Hello everyone! *(audience response)* hang on am I facing the right way? I said hello everyone! *(audience response)*. That's much better now allow me to introduce myself, my name is Duchess Dolly Delilah Dollop and I live here in Wonderland with my adopted son Wally the White Rabbit, I adopted him when he was just a tiny little bunny! But that boy is always late!

However, that boy's lateness is the least of my worries! Things aren't going well here in Wonderland, and worst of all I'm single! That's right I'm young, single and ready to mingle… Well I'm single and ready to mingle! Let's have a look at some of our newest residents of Wonderland shall we? *(DUCHESS to improvise with a few men on the front row, flirting with them etc and finally picking one man to be her new boyfriend for the rest of the show)*. Now that I've made sure this man will be getting every penny of his ticket this evening, I'll carry on with the rest of the script! That's right there's actually a script, someone wrote this rubbish!

As I was saying before I got distracted by all of these gorgeous men who made the mistake of sitting on the front row, Wonderland is in trouble, you see we're currently ruled by the evil Queen of Hearts, she's banned all fun around here in Wonderland, if you so much as whistle she'll have you executed! She's making life miserable for all of us here in Wonderland! She's so mean!

She's so mean she makes the Grinch seem kind!

She's so mean she makes the Evil Queen from Snow White seem nice!

In fact she's so mean she makes a Conservative government look like they care!

She's sooooooo mean- Well I think you get the picture she's horrible! And she's a proper minger as well, when she was a baby, they put the nappy on the wrong end!

Now then everyone before I forget, I've been doing some baking here in Wonderland I've made a lovely custard pie! *(a big custard pie is handed on from the wings)*. Now I'm going to leave this custard pie on the side over here and if anyone goes to take it can shout 'leave the pie alone' *(audience response)*, well, can you? *(audience response)*, good let's give it a go, I'm going to go off and then I'll come back on pretending to be someone else who wants to take the pie! *(DUCHESS goes off and sneaks towards the pie. Audience: leave the pie alone!)* You'll have to be a lot louder than that, I'm deaf in one eye! *(Duchess goes off and sneaks towards the pie again. Audience: leave the pie alone!)* Well, that was a bit better, but I think we can be even louder ready one last time *(DUCHESS goes off and sneaks towards the pie again. Audience: leave the pie alone!)* That's much better, now I know my pie is in safe hands.

QUEEN: *(From offstage)* Off with their heads!

DUCHESS: Oh no here comes that horrible Queen of Hearts now, don't forget to give her a big boo when she comes out! I'm out of here before she decides she wants to chop my head off! See you all later boys and girls! Bye! *(Exit DUCHESS)*

(Enter the QUEEN OF HEARTS)

QUEEN: Where is everybody! I'm very bored… Oh hang on there's loads of you out here! *(sniffs)* what's that smell… *(sniffs again. Recoils in horror)* Ugh! It's common people! What are all you common people doing here? *(Points to someone in the audience)* You! Stand up! What is your name *(audience member responds)* Well *(insert audience members name here)* and where are you from? *(audience member responds)* Ugh! And where is that? *(audience member responds)* That doesn't sound like Wonderland to me! But I think you have a nice smile, even if it is ugly, you may sit! *(Points to another member of the audience)* You! Stand up! What is your name? *(interrupts them)* I don't care. What is your job? *(interrupts them again)* I don't care. Sit. I'm done with you. And you *(points to another member of the audience though this audience member is a stooge)* You! Stand up!

What is your name? *(audience members response. THE QUEEN flies into a rage.)* THAT IS AN AWFUL NAME! I HATE THAT NAME! I HATE IT! I HATE IT! I HATE IT! I HATE IT! Guards! Guards! *(several playing cards who are the*

Queens guards appear) Arrest that man! *(The guards go into the audience and grab the audience member and drag them backstage)* AND OFF WITH HIS HEAD! I really didn't like his name… Though I can't remember what it was! Oh well, off with his head! OFF WITH HIS HEAD! In fact, off with all of your heads! That's right all of you! I don't like any of you!

(As the QUEEN begins to fly into what seems to be an even bigger tantrum the KING, a bumbling man runs on with a plate of jam tarts to calm the QUEEN down)

KING: Now, now my dear look a jam tart, you like jam tarts *(He begins to shovel them into the QUEENS mouth.)* That's it let's both calm down-

QUEEN: *(Spitting jam tart all over the KING)* DON'T TELL ME TO CALM DOWN! I AM CALM!

KING: Yes my love of course you are, you're very calm. One of the calmest people I know!

QUEEN: It wasn't my fault it was… Well I can't remember his name, but it was a stupid name and I hated it! And on top of that all of these common people seem to keep booing me and I HATE IT! DON'T BOO ME OR I SHALL HAVE ALL OF YOUR HEADS CHOPPED OFF!

KING: Another jam tart my love?

QUEEN: Yes please… *(takes a bite)* Hang on this one isn't jam it's lemon!

(Before the QUEEN can shout at the KING again, the KING puts a jam tart into her mouth as she goes to shout)

KING: My apologies my love. Now what say we get you back to the castle.

QUEEN: Will there be jam tarts?

KING: Yes, yes, lots of jam tarts!

QUEEN: Good. I'm not in a very good mood. Can we chop off someone's head as well?

KING: Yes of course we can.

QUEEN: Good. I'm feeling much better already.

KING: Anything for you my love

Song 2 – KING and QUEEN of Hearts

(The KING and QUEEN of Hearts exit off after there song arm in arm. Enter ALICE and WALLY)

WALLY: What time is it? *(Audience: You're late!)*

ALICE: What a thoroughly horrible woman!

WALLY: That's the Queen of Hearts, she's so horrid, a proper baddie, she rules Wonderland with an iron fist and if you don't like what she says that's it! Off with your head!

ALICE: That's barbaric!

(Enter DUCHESS)

DUCHESS: There you are Wally! Oh, and who's this with you?

ALICE: My name's Alice and I'm new here to Wonderland!

DUCHESS: How did you get in, I went down the rabbit whole!

DUCHESS: And what about this lot out here?

WALLY: They've paid to come in-

DUCHESS: Feels like a waste of money to me.

WALLY: That's what I said.

ALICE: Why do you put up with that awful Queen-

DUCHESS: You can't say that about me!

WALLY: She means the Queen of Hearts Mum!

DUCHESS: Oh yes that does make more sense. Well there's not much we can do, if we try anything she'll have us executed!

WALLY: Yeah, and I like my head attached to my neck thank you very much!

ALICE: But what about if everyone in Wonderland stood up to her. You could live freely and have fun without her ruling over you all!

WALLY: That sounds risky to me-

ALICE: Surely the risk is worth it to save the whole of Wonderland?

DUCHESS: I think she could be right Wally! We can travel the whole of Wonderland and convince everyone to stand up to the Queen.

WALLY: I suppose she can't execute all of us!

ALICE: So, it's settled then!

WALLY: I know who we can go and see first!

ALICE: Who's that?

WALLY: The Caterpillar!

ALICE: A caterpillar? What use is a caterpillar?

DUCHESS: Everyone is of use here in Wonderland!

ALICE: But a caterpillar is so small! How would we even approach a creature who is only three inches tall?

WALLY: Easy, we shrink down to their size!

ALICE: How?

DUCHESS: *(Pulls out three bottles each with a label that reads 'Drink This')* We drink these and we'll shrink down to the size of a caterpillar.

ALICE: Okay, so it's decided we'll travel Wonderland meeting everyone and getting them onside and then finally all together we'll defeat the Queen of Hearts and restore happiness to Wonderland!

Song 3 – DUCHESS, WALLY and ALICE

(At the end of the song the DUCHESS, WALLY and ALICE drink the bottles reading 'drink me' and shrink. When they shrink they become small versions of themselves as puppets. The following dialogue is performed by the puppet versions of ALICE, DUCHESS and WALLY)

DUCHESS: Does anyone else feel a bit weird?

ALICE: I feel very strange!

WALLY: Come on, let's go and find the Caterpillar!

(Blackout)

SCENE TWO

THE CATERPILLAR'S LEAF

Song 4 – CATERPILLAR & the FIREFLIES

(Enter ALICE, WALLY and DUCHESS)

WALLY: What time is it? *(Audience: you're late!)*

CATERPILLAR: Who are you?

ALICE: My name is Alice, and this is Duchess Dolly and Wally the White Rabbit.

CATERPILLAR: Yes, those are your names… But who are you?

DUCHESS: She just said she's Alice, I'm Duchess Dolly and this is Wally the White Rabbit-

CATERPILLAR: Yes, yes. I know your names. But I don't know anything about you, where did you come from, why are you here? What do you want from me? And why are you all only three inches tall?

ALICE: We're not really three inches tall-

CATERPILLAR: A fine size is three inches.

DUCHESS: I've heard that before.

CATERPILLAR: But tell me do you like poetry?

WALLY: This is getting a bit weird…

CATERPILLAR: I shall recite to you a poem-

DUCHESS: We only really came here to ask-

CATERPILLAR: Well listen and it shall be answered-

WALLY: But we haven't asked yet!

CATERPILLAR: How doth the little crocodile
    Improve his shining tail,
    And pour the waters of the Nile
    On every golden scale!
    How cheerfully he seems to grin,
    How neatly spreads his claws,
    And welcomes little fishes in
    With gently smiling jaws!

ALICE: That's not how I remember it.

DUCHESS: Well, that's what it says in the script-

WALLY: I've got a poem!

> Betty Botter bought some butter
> But she said the butter's bitter
> If I put it in my batter, it will make my batter bitter
> But a bit of better butter will make my batter better
> So 'twas better Betty Botter bought a bit of better butter

DUCHESS: So I do I,

> I am not the pheasant plucker,
> I'm the pheasant plucker's mate.
> I am only plucking pheasants
> Because the pheasant plucker's late.

WALLY: I bet you can't say that again! But much faster!

DUCHESS: *(Said with some pace)*

> I am not the pheasant plucker,
> I'm the pheasant plucker's mate.
> I am only plucking pheasants
> Because the pheasant plucker's late.

CATERPILLAR: Very Good, but what about,

> I'm not the fig plucker,
> Nor the fig plucker's son,
> But I'll pluck figs
> Till the fig plucker comes.

(ALICE, DUCHESS, and WALLY all give the CATERPILLAR a round of applause)

Thank you. Now what is your reason for coming here as much as I do love poetry, I'm a very busy bee-

WALLY: Really, I thought you were a Caterpillar?

ALICE: We're here to recruit you to stand up to the Queen of Hearts!

CATERPILLAR: Stand up and fight the Queen of Hearts. Well, I suppose it would make me a lot happier! But what can we do at only three inches tall?

WALLY: We're not normally this small. We can grow back to our normal size-

DUCHESS: Ah.

WALLY: What do you mean ah? Are we stuck at three inches tall forever?

DUCHESS: I've forgotten to bring the bottle with me that changes us back to being big again!

CATERPILLAR: Well one side will make you grow taller, and one side will make you grow shorter!

ALICE: The other side of what?

CATERPILLAR: Why this mushroom of course! *(CATERPILLAR points to the giant mushroom)*

DUCHESS: Is it left or right to grow taller?

CATERPILLAR: One side for taller, one side for shorter-

DUCHESS: Yes, but which side is which?

CATERPILLAR: The left. Try the left.

(DUCHESS, ALICE and WALLY all eat the left side of the Mushroom and the lights begin to flash and flicker as they all begin to grow back to normal size. The leaf that was once huge is now a tiny leaf)

ALICE: Where did the Caterpillar go?

(CATERPILLAR enters now as a Butterfly)

CATERPILLAR: Do you mean me? And as for your quest when I am needed, I shall be there, but as for now I shall fly away!

(CATERPILLAR flutters off. Exit CATERPILLAR)

ALICE: Well which way do we go now?

WALLY & DUCHESS: This way *(Both pointing in different directions)* That way *(Again both pointing in different directions)*

ALICE: What about this way.

(Exit ALICE, WALLY and DUCHESS through the auditorium. Blackout onstage)

SCENE THREE

TWEEDLE DEE AND TWEEDLE DUM'S COTTAGE

Song 5 – TWEEDLE DEE and TWEEDLE DUM

(At the end of the song TWEEDLE DEE and TWEEDLE DUM stand frozen. Enter ALICE.)

ALICE: Why, what peculiar little figures *(she pokes one of the statues in the belly)*

DEE: If you think we're waxworks you'll have to pay you know!

DUM: And if you think we're alive you'll have to speak to us!

(DEE & DUM perform a TikTok dance)

DEE & DUM: That's logic!

ALICE: Well, it was nice meeting you!

DEE & DUM: Don't go yet! Join in with us!

ALICE: But how would I join in with you?

DEE: It's easy!

DUM: You just Tik!

DEE: Then you Tok!

ALICE: TikTok?

(ALICE, DEE and DUM perform a TikTok dance)

ALICE: That was easy!

DEE: Everything's easy when you Tik

DUM: And Tok!

(ALICE, DEE and DUM perform another TikTok dance.)

DUM: Hang on a minute!

DEE: What's that custard pie doing over there!

(DEE & DUM both move towards the custard pie. Audience: leave the pie alone!)

(Enter DUCHESS)

DUCHESS: Get your hands off my pie!

DEE & DUM: Your pie?

DUCHESS: Yes, my pie!

(Enter WALLY)

WALLY: What time is it?

(AUDIENCE: You're late!)

DUCHESS: I told you we'd be late if we didn't follow Alice! Now what's going on here?

DEE & DUM: TikTok

(DUCHESS, WALLY, ALICE, DEE and DUM perform a TikTok dance)

WALLY: That was brilliant! Can we do it again?

DUCHESS: No, I don't think anyone wants to see us do another TikTok!

DEE & DUM: TikTok!

(DUCHESS, WALLY, ALICE, DEE and DUM perform another TikTok dance)

ALICE: We're actually a bit lost!

DEE: Well, we can help you there!

DUM: We know where to go!

DUCHESS: I swear if one of you says TikTok again I'll whack you!

DEE & DUM: TikTok!

(DUCHESS, WALLY, ALICE, DEE and DUM perform a TikTok dance)

DUCHESS: That's the last time! Look at all the grown ups out there they haven't got a clue what's going on!

ALICE: You said you could help us.

DEE: Well, that depends.

DUM: On where you're going!

WALLY: Well, we're sort of just rounding people up to take on that evil Queen of Hearts, so we can live happily again!

DUM: And you'd like our help?

DEE: You want us to help you take on the Queen of Hearts?

ALICE: Yes please!

DEE & DUM: *(Look at one another and then turn back to ALICE)* Then our help you shall have!

WALLY: Great! Now how do we get out of here?

(There is a crashing sound, and the stage goes dark)

ALICE: What was that?

DEE & DUM: Nights fallen.

WALLY: I don't like it here it's getting a bit spooky!

DEE: It's supposed to be haunted!

DUCHESS: Haunted?

DUM: Yes haunted!

DEE: By ghosties!

DUM: And ghoulies!

DUCHESS: Well, I don't want to get grabbed by the ghosties!

WALLY: And I don't want grabbed by the-

ALL: Wally!

DUCHESS: Well, I'm sure if the boys and girls see something strange they'll shout out, won't you boys and girls?

(audience response)

WALLY: Yes, you'll tell us if you see anything won't you boys and girls! *(Audience response)*

ALICE: I'm getting a bit scared.

DUCHESS: Don't worry Alice, we can sing a song to keep us safe!

WALLY: What song shall we sing?

DEE & DUM: What about…

Song 6 – ALICE, DUCHESS, WALLY, DEE & DUM

(As they sing a GHOST appears behind them)

WALLY: What was it?

AUDIENCE: A ghost!

DUCHESS: A ghost?

WALLY: A ghost!

DEE & DUM: A ghost!

ALICE: A ghost!

ALL: A ghost! Well we'll have to sing it again then won't we, whoops!

Song 6a – ALICE, DUCHESS, WALLY, DEE & DUM

(As they sing a GHOST appears behind them)

WALLY: What was it?

AUDIENCE: A ghost!

DUCHESS: A ghost?

WALLY: A ghost!

DEE & DUM: A ghost!

ALICE: *(The GHOST taps ALICE on the shoulder)* A ghost! (*ALICE* is chased off by the *GHOST*)

WALLY: Hang on where's Alice gone?

AUDIENCE: The ghost took her etc

WALLY: The ghost took her?

DUCHESS, WALLY, DEE AND DUM: Well, we'll have to sing it again then won't we, whoops!

Song 6b – DUCHESS, WALLY, DEE & DUM

(As they sing a GHOST appears behind them)

WALLY: What was it?

AUDIENCE: A ghost!

DUCHESS: A ghost?

WALLY: A ghost!

DEE & DUM: *(The GHOST taps DEE and DUM on the shoulders)* A ghost! (*ALICE* is chased off by the *GHOST*)

WALLY: Hang on where's Tweedle Dee and Tweedle Dum gone?

AUDIENCE: The ghost took them etc

WALLY: The ghost took them?

DUCHESS & WALLY: Well, we'll have to sing it again then won't we, whoops!

Song 6c – DUCHESS & WALLY

(As they sing a GHOST appears behind them)

WALLY: What was it?

AUDIENCE: A ghost!

DUCHESS: A Ghost?

WALLY: *(The GHOST taps WALLY on the shoulders)* A ghost! *(ALICE is chased off by the GHOST)*

DUCHESS: Hang on where's Wally gone?

AUDIENCE: The ghost took him etc

DUCHESS: The ghost took them? Well, I'll have to sing it again then won't I, whoops!

Song 6d – DUCHESS & WALLY

(As she sings a GHOST appears behind her)

DUCHESS: What is it?

AUDIENCE: A ghost!

DUCHESS: A ghost? Let me just have a look then *(the DUCHESS sneaks around with the ghost following her)*. There's nothing there! *(audience response)* Oh no there isn't! *(Audience: oh yes there is!)* Oh no there isn't! *(Audience: oh yes there is!)* Oh no there isn't! *(Audience: oh yes there is!)*

(The GHOST now holds DUCHESS'S hand. The DUCHESS doesn't look at who is holding her hand.)

Oh, *(insert name of the man she picked on at the start of the show)* I'm so glad you've decided to join me onstage, I've been so very frightened! *(noticing that her man is still sat down in the audience)* Hang on a minute, if you're sat down there… Then who's holding my hand. *(DUCHESS and the GHOST both look at one another. The ghost screams and runs off)*

Charming!

(Blackout)

SCENE FOUR

WONDERLAND SHOW BAR

(From the Blackout we hear a strange voice, it's the CHESHIRE CAT. During the blackout the scene is changed to the Wonderland Show Bar, a 1920s style speakeasy)

CAT: Hey all you cool cats, it's me baby the coolest cat of them all the Cheshire Cat. I'm styling, smiling and profiling baby. And I'd like to welcome you to the Wonderland Show Bar the hippest bar in Wonderland where all the cool cats play. And now I present to you the ever-famous Cheshire Cat Cabaret. Let's get some lights on me. *(Spot on the CHESHIRE CAT)* Music!

Song 7 – CHESHIRE CAT & CAST

(Song finishes)

CAT: Thanks everyone and now a special treat for you performing live please welcome to the Wonderland stage the Dodo and the Duck!

DODO: You may think I'm extinct but, let me tell you the same thing I told the Duck. The Dodo never dies and sometimes it even flies.

DUCK: And now you're in luck because it's the dynamic duo of the Dodo and the Duck! So, let's see you thriving, surviving and hand jiving because here we go!

Song 8 – DODO, DUCK and CAST

CAT: Alright you crazy cats, we're gonna take five! So, make sure you look alive, cos here at Wonderland we're only just starting to jive!

(Enter ALICE, WALLY and DUCHESS)

WALLY: What time is it? *(Audience: you're late)*

ALICE: Who are we here to see?

WALLY: The Cheshire Cat

DUCHESS: Yeah, if we get him onside, I reckon a few more will join our cause!

ALICE: I wonder where he could be.

CAT: Hey there little Miss and what might your name be?

ALICE: My name's Alice-

CAT: Alice, a pleasure to make your acquaintance baby. I'm the Cheshire Cat and I run this bar. The coolest bar in all of Wonderland!

WALLY: Well, that was easy.

DUCHESS: What was easy?

WALLY: Finding the Cheshire Cat

CAT: And why might you want to find little old me? *(Sees DUCHESS)* Well hold on just a second who might this fine slice of woman be? *(Kissing DUCHESS on the hand)*

DUCHESS: *(Giggles)* Oh! You mean me? Well, I'm flattered I must say!

WALLY: Yeah, and he must be confused or mad.

CAT: We're all mad here. I'm mad. *(to ALICE)* You're mad.

ALICE: How do you know I'm mad?

CAT: You must be, or you wouldn't have come here. *(To DUCHESS)* We don't get many women like you in here-

WALLY: You're not wrong!

CAT: The moment I saw you I was entranced!

WALLY: You'll be horrified if you take her home-

DUCHESS: Be quiet Wally! *(Clips him round the ear)*.

ALICE: Excuse me Mr. Cat?

CAT: Yes, little lady?

ALICE: We were wondering if you'd join us in taking on the Queen of Hearts *(everyone in the Wonderland Bar gasps and the room goes quiet)*

CAT: Take on the Queen, why she's the reason the Wonderland Show Bar is kept a secret!

DUCHESS: It can't be that secret, I mean we just walked in. You're hardly inconspicuous yourself a walking talking-

CAT: And singing, don't forget singing baby!

DUCHESS: Cat!

CAT: But without that mean Queen ruling us we'd be free to party all the time! We wouldn't have to hide every time there's a spot check by her guards!

DODO: *(Shouts from the back)* The guards are coming!

(Everyone frantically clears away the Wonderland Show Bar and hides. The CAT and ALICE put lampshades on their heads and pretend to be lamps, the DODO hides behind a newspaper and WALLY and the DUCHESS hide in the audience. Everyone else either runs offstage or finds a hiding place)

(Enter the Playing Card GUARDS)

TWO OF DIAMONDS: Now what's going on here?

THREE OF DIAMONDS: Were those lamps always there!

DUCHESS: *(From the audience)* Yes!

TWO OF DIAMONDS: And who are you?

WALLY: We're just the audience!

THREE OF DIAMONDS: Very well.

(Exit GUARDS. Everyone comes out from their hiding places and sets the bar back up, just as it's set up the DODO shouts once again)

DODO: The guards are coming back! *(Everyone goes back to where they were hidden the first time. As well as clearing the bar away once again)*

(Enter GUARDS)

TWO OF DIAMONDS: Thought I saw something!

WALLY: *(From the audience)* Nope! Nothing here but us audience members!

THREE OF DIAMONDS: Fair enough, come on let's get back to the castle! I hear the Queen is going to play some croquet!

(Exit GUARDS. Everyone comes out from their hiding places and sets the bar back up)

WALLY: You do that every time the guards come through here?

CAT: Yeah, baby or we might lose our heads!

DODO: The guards are coming!

DUCHESS: What again? You must be joking!

> *(Everyone goes back to where they were hidden the first time again. As well as clearing the bar away once again. Enter GUARDS.)*

TWO OF DIAMONDS: I'm sure we've been this way before

WALLY: *(From the audience)* You have!

THREE OF DIAMONDS: Have we?

DUCHESS: *(From the audience)* Yes, now clear off!

TWO OF DIAMONDS: Who said that?

DUCHESS: *(From the audience)* We did. They've- I mean we've not paid ten pound a ticket for this rubbish!

THREE OF DIAMONDS: Fair enough. There's nothing going on here anyway!

> *(Exit GUARDS. Everyone comes out from their hiding places and sets the bar back up)*

CAT: I think I speak for all of us here when I say we'll happily join your cause to take down the Queen of Hearts-

DODO: The guards are coming-

DUCHESS: No! No, they're not I can't do all that running around again! I mean look at him over there, he's had to take that table on and off three times, you're going to kill the poor man!

DODO: Oh no false alarm!

DUCHESS: I should think so!

WALLY: Will you help us out Mr. Cat?

CAT: Of course, baby!

DODO: I will too!

DUCK: And me!

ENSEMBLE: Us too!

ALICE: That's wonderful news!

CAT: When you need us, we'll be there to lend a helping paw!

DUCK: Or feather!

ALICE: Thank you so much! Who should we ask next?

CAT: Oh, you want to go and see the Mad Hatter, he's due to celebrate his unbirthday at his next tea party baby!

DODO: Yeah, if you get the Mad Hatter, you'll also get the Dormouse and the March Hare!

ALICE: That's great news? What's he like?

DUCK: He's mad of course!

ALICE: Well, it looks like we've a tea party to attend!

(Blackout)

SCENE FIVE

QUEEN OF HEARTS CASTLE

(Lights up. The QUEEN is sat on her throne)

QUEEN: Hello everyone, it's me again! Did you miss me? *(audience response)* Oh shut up I don't care anyway! I'm very bored! I'm bored! Oh, look it's all the commoners back again, you shall cure my boredom for now. What are you still doing here? JAM TARTS! I WANT JAM TARTS NOW!

(Enter KING with a plate of Jam Tarts he frantically pushes them into the QUEENS mouth)

KING: There there do calm down my love-

QUEEN: I am calm! It was all of the commoners sat out there annoying me again! Look at them all, they're all so ugly and disgusting, sitting there stuffing their faces with sweets they've bought before the show! No class at all! *(The QUEEN shovels more jam tarts into her mouth until the plate is empty)* MORE JAM TARTS!

KING: Right away my love! *(Exit KING)*

QUEEN: Hurry up! I want my tarts and I want them now!

(Enter KING)

KING: It seems we have none left my love…

QUEEN: What?

KING: You've eaten them all-

QUEEN: Oh no I haven't!

KING: Oh yes you have!

QUEEN: Oh no I haven't!

KING: Oh yes you have!

QUEEN: Oh no I haven't!

KING: Oh yes you have!

QUEEN: Oh, be quiet! I can't have eaten all of the jam tarts! I know what's happened!

KING: You do?

QUEEN: Someone has stolen my jam tarts.

KING: I think it really might just be that you've eaten them all-

QUEEN: WHO DARES STEAL MY JAM TARTS! GUARDS GET IN HERE IMMEDIATELY! *(Enter GUARDS. Several playing cards enter)* I believe one of you has stolen my jam tarts! *(points to the seven of spades)* Did you steal my tarts?

SEVEN OF SPADES: No, your majesty.

QUEEN: *(pointing at the FOUR OF CLUBS)* Did you steal my tarts?

FOUR OF CLUBS: No, your majesty.

QUEEN: *(pointing at the NINE OF HEARTS)* Did you steal my tarts?

NINE OF HEARTS: No, your majesty.

QUEEN: *(Points to an audience member)* You! Did you steal my tarts? *(audience member response. Points to a different audience member)* You! Did you steal my tarts? *(audience member response. Points to another audience member)* You! Did you steal my tarts? *(audience member response)*. Someone here is lying. And when I find out who it is heads will roll!

Song 9 – QUEEN, KING and the GUARDS

(At the end of the song the QUEEN has found out that it is the FOUR OF CLUBS has allegedly stolen the jam tarts)

QUEEN: *(To the FOUR OF CLUBS)* YOU. STOLE. MY. JAM. TARTS. OFF WITH THEIR HEAD! I SAID OFF WITH THEIR HEAD! GUARDS! GUARDS! TAKE THEM AWAY AND OFF WITH THEIR HEAD IMMEDIATELY!

FOUR OF CLUBS: I promise I didn't steal your jam tarts!

QUEEN: And why should I believe you?

FOUR OF CLUBS: Because I don't like jam!

QUEEN: Lies! Now stop grovelling, I know it was you! OFF WITH HIS HEAD!

FOUR OF CLUBS: Please have mercy your majesty!

QUEEN: Mercy? *(Laughs)* NO! OFF WITH HIS HEAD!

FOUR OF CLUBS: *(As he is being dragged away)* You won't get away with this!

(The GUARDS drag off the FOUR OF CLUBS)

QUEEN: And all of you lot can shut up as well! Or I'll have you all executed! In fact, off with all of your heads! That's right all of you! Off with all of your heads!

KING: Why don't we go and have a game of croquet instead?

QUEEN: What?

KING: Let's go and have a nice game of croquet and the cook has said he'll have more jam tarts for you very soon.

QUEEN: Croquet and jam tarts?

KING: Anything for you my love

QUEEN: Fine. *(To the audience)* You're lucky I'm in a good mood!

(Exit KING and QUEEN)

(Blackout)

SCENE SIX

THE MAD HATTERS HOUSE

> *(Lights up on the Mad Hatters tea party we see a long table covered with cakes, tea pots and cups of tea with the MAD HATTER, DORMOUSE and MARCH HARE sat at the table)*

HATTER: Well, hello everyone out there and welcome to my unbirthday celebrations!

HARE: I thought it was my unbirthday?

DORMOUSE: But I thought it was my unbirthday too!

HATTER: But it can't be all of our unbirthdays… For surely, it's not our birthdays?

DORMOUSE: That doesn't make sense!

HATTER: Does it need too?

> *(They all fall about laughing)*

HATTER: More tea?

DORMOUSE: For me?

HARE: And me?

> *(The HATTER pours out some tea for the MARCH HARE and the DORMOUSE)*

HARE & DORMOUSE: Cheers!

DORMOUSE: But what about some cake?

HARE: Or a nice custard pie!

HATTER: I say we don't seem to have any custard pies!

DORMOUSE: What about that custard pie over there *(pointing to the DUCHESS'S custard pie on the side of the stage)*

HATTER: Why that pie looks delicious! *(Goes towards the pie. Audience: leave the pie alone! Enter DUCHESS followed by ALICE and WALLY)*

DUCHESS: Oi hands off my pie!

HATTER: Your pie?

DUCHESS: Yes, my pie!

HATTER: That's alright we have plenty of pies here anyway! Would you like some tea!

DORMOUSE & HARE: More Tea!

ALICE: Are you having some kind of party?

HATTER: Yes, it's my unbirthday!

HARE: And mine!

DORMOUSE: Mine too!

ALICE: What's an unbirthday?

HATTER: We don't know! *(DORMOUSE, HARE and HATTER all fall about laughing)*

ALICE: You're entirely bonkers!

HATTER: Let me tell you, all the best people are! Now would you like some tea?

HARE: And some cake?

DORMOUSE: I'd love some cake!

HARE: Here have a pie! *(Hare shoves a pie in the DORMOUSE'S face)*

DORMOUSE: Banana Cream my favourite!

HARE: Can I have a pie?

DORMOUSE: Of course you can! Here! *(DORMOUSE pushes a pie into the MARCH HARE'S face)*

HATTER: I'll give you both some tea! *(The HATTER throws a cup of tea in both the HARE and DORMOUSE'S faces)*

HARE: That was delightfully refreshing! Thank you!

DORMOUSE: May I have another?

HATTER: Why of course! *(Throws another cup of tea in the DORMOUSE'S face)*. Would any of you like some tea?

WALLY: Well, I wouldn't mind a custard pie I suppose!

(The HATTER, DORMOUSE and HARE pick up a custard pie each)

HATTER: Shall we let him have it boys and girls? *(audience response)* Very well! Here you go! *(HATTER, DORMOUSE and HARE all push a pie into the face of WALLY)*

WALLY: Thanks! Now some tea please!

(DORMOUSE, HARE and HATTER all throw a cup of tea at WALLY)

HATTER: Hang on just a minute I haven't had any cake or tea?

WALLY: *(WALLY pushes a pie into the HATTER'S face)* There you go!

HATTER: But what about my tea?

HARE: Here you go! *(Throws a cup of tea into the HATTERS face)*

HATTER: Oh, now this tea doesn't have any sugar in it!

HARE: Terribly sorry about that, how's this one? *(HARE throws another cup of tea in the HATTER'S face)*

HATTER: Ah, yes! Much better thank you! A fine cup of tea!

DUCHESS: Oh, look a plate of marshmallows! I do love a marshmallow!

HATTER: Have as many as you like! I have a magic plate where you can eat as many marshmallows are you want! Look there's only one on this plate why not eat it!

DUCHESS: Do you know what I think I will! *(DUCHESS puts the marshmallow in here mouth and eats it)*

HATTER: How about some more? *(HATTER gets another plate of marshmallows this time there are three marshmallows on the plate)*

DUCHESS: I couldn't possibly!

HATTER: It'd be rude not too!

DUCHESS: Well, I don't want to be rude! *(DUCHESS shoves all three marshmallows in her mouth)*

HARE & DORMOUSE: More marshmallows!

DUCHESS: *(Still with marshmallows in her mouth)* What?!

HATTER: Yes, here, there are more on this plate! In fact, there are more than we practised with in rehearsals! Eat up you wouldn't want to be rude!

(DUCHESS shoves all of the marshmallows in her mouth)

HATTER: What do you think boys and girls should she have some more marshmallows! *(audience response)*

DUCHESS: *(With Marshmallows in her mouth)* No!

HATTER: *(With another plate of Marshmallows)* Go on you wouldn't want to be rude!

DUCHESS: *(Piles the rest of the Marshmallows in her mouth)*

HATTER: Do you know I think I can magically make those marshmallows reappear!

WALLY: I don't think it'll take much!

(The DUCHESS waves to the side of the stage and one of the stage crew walks onstage with a plastic bag and the DUCHESS spits out all of the marshmallows into the bag slowly to get a reaction from the audience)

WALLY: *(To the stagehand)* I bet you didn't think you'd get a starring role in this show did you!

DUCHESS: He nearly had to call an ambulance!

(The crew member tries to walk off, however the DUCHESS grabs him)

DUCHESS: Before you go would you like a custard pie?

CREW MEMBER: No-

WALLY: Come on kids who thinks *(insert stage crew members name)* should have a custard pie before he goes? *(audience response. WALLY hands DUCHESS a pie)*

DUCHESS: Now shall I let him have it? *(audience response. DUCHESS pushes the pie into the stage crew members face. Crew member wipes his eyes and walks off)*. Give him a big cheer everyone! Now where were we?

WALLY: At this point I have no idea!

ALICE: Well, I'd like the Hatter, Dormouse and March Hare to come and help us defeat the Queen?

WALLY: Oh, we're going back to the script now are we?

DUCHESS: There's a script this year is there?

WALLY: Hang on Alice hasn't had any pie?

ALICE: That's fine I don't want any!

HATTER: Are you sure Alice it's delicious!

ALICE: I'm quite sure thank you.

DORMOUSE: What about some tea?

ALICE: Tea would be lovely though I'd prefer it in a cup rather than thrown at me please.

HATTER: Very well, here is your tea *(Hands ALICE a cup of tea).* Now Alice tell me Why is a Raven like a writing desk?

ALICE: I don't know!

HATTER: Neither do I that's why I'm asking you!

DUCHESS: *(Looking at her teacup)* I'm starting to think there's more than just tea in here.

HATTER: No, my dear woman, nothing more than a splash of tea for you and me! Now Alice tell us why have you come here?

ALICE: Well, you see we need your help.

HARE & DORMOUSE: And ours?

ALICE: Yes, all three of you! You see we want to defeat the Queen of Hearts and make Wonderland a fun place again that isn't ruled by fear!

HATTER: Then we might perhaps have even bigger tea parties!

ALICE: Well yes of course you could!

HATTER: Tea and cake for everyone!

DORMOUSE: Hang on *(looking at the audience)* this lot out here haven't had any tea or cake?

HARE: Then we should let them have some

WALLY: Are you saying we should let them have it?

HATTER: My dear boy that's exactly what we're saying! Tea and cake for everyone!

(DORMOUSE and HARE pull out two super soakers labelled 'tea' and begin to squirt the audience. WALLY and the

DUCHESS go down into the audience with a custard pie each and dab bits of the custard pie on audience members faces. The HATTER throws out giant inflatable doughnuts into the audience. ALICE sits drinking tea during the ongoing madness)

HATTER: Right, I think that's quite enough tea and cake for everyone!

(All come back to stage and sit up the table. The MAD HATTER stands.)

HATTER: Now Alice to answer your question. Yes, we will help you out in defeating the Queen of Hearts and then we'll throw the biggest Unbirthday party ever! But right now, we do need to tidy up!

DORMOUSE: How long will that take?

WALLY: I'd imagine about fifteen to twenty minutes. *(Winks at the audience. Blackout)*

CAT: *(As a Voice-over)* That's the end of Act One all you cool cats, so while we tidy up, go get yourself a drink, or nip to the loo if that's what you need to do! We'll see you back in Wonderland for more fun and madness in Act Two!

(Interval)

ACT TWO

SCENE ONE

THE QUEEN OF HEARTS CASTLE

Song 10 – QUEEN OF HEARTS & CARDS

(The song finishes with the QUEEN standing triumphant with her GUARDS)

QUEEN: JAM TARTS! I WANT MY JAM TARTS!

(Enter KING. Who runs on with a plate of Jam Tarts)

AND EVERYONE ELSE GET OUT!

(GUARDS leave in a hurry)

KING: Jam Tart my love?

QUEEN: Yes please. *(The QUEEN opens her mouth, and the KING begins feeding her jam tarts)*

(Enter KNAVE OF HEARTS)

KNAVE: Your Majesty *(he bows)*

QUEEN: Oh hello. What are you doing here?

KNAVE: Well your majesty I have come to tell you some news.

QUEEN: Is it good news?

KNAVE: No, your majesty.

QUEEN: I don't like bad news and I was in such a good mood until now.

KNAVE: Well-

QUEEN: No wait. Tell me the news via song.

KNAVE: You want me to sing you the news?

QUEEN: Yes, and quickly as I'm getting bored! Music!

Song 11 – Song About Alice (to the tune of Modern Major General) – KNAVE OF HEARTS

There is a girl called Alice, who came here through a rabbit hole
She's blonde and wears a dress and her speaking is impeccable.
She's made a few new friends and is causing quite a major scene
Saying as a Queen you seem too just be mean

I'm very well aware that this doesn't sound too practical.
I understand you may be mad, but it doesn't matter not at all
She's building up an army and it's your royal reign she wants to end!
She really doesn't like you, no not at all it seems.
It looks as though the Hatter has come along to join the cause.
Can we stop this song it's far too fast and I need to pause

In short, this song is far too long, it seems to just be going on
You're looking like you need a tart or even just a nap

There is a rising happening, it came here through a rabbit hole
It's blonde and wears a dress and it's speaking is impeccable.
She's making brand new friends and is causing quite a major fuss
Saying as a Queen you seem to be a little sus

Hang on let me check to see now if I have got that all
It simply seems to me that you're in for a mega fall.
Yes it seems to me like you're in for a mega brawl.
With absolutely anyone and everyone and anything

There's no more news to tell you now
I think I should get gone some how
And also, is it getting hot?
My stomach's tying in a knot
I'm going, gone, I'm on the run
This job has never been that fun
I wish you all the best I do Goodbye you!

I'm off!

(KNAVE goes to exit)

QUEEN: Hold it right there!

KNAVE: Please your majesty don't shoot the messenger!

QUEEN: Shoot you? Why would I shoot you?

KNAVE: Phew!

QUEEN: When I can CHOP OF YOUR HEAD INSTEAD! OFF
    WITH HIS HEAD! OFF WITH HIS HEAD I SAY!

KNAVE: Please your majesty!

QUEEN: I don't like receiving bad news! You've totally ruined my
    day! OFF WITH HIS HEAD!

KING: My love if I could just intervene for a second-

QUEEN: What is it?

KING: Well with the inevitable uprising happening with this Alice girl we might be seen more favourably if we were to put the Knave of Hearts on trial.

QUEEN: Then after the trial can we chop his head off?

KNAVE: But I haven't done anything wrong! I've only told you bad news.

QUEEN: I suppose not… But you have been stealing my jam tarts! And that is a crime punishable by BEHEADING!

KNAVE: I haven't stolen any of your tarts.

QUEEN: Well, I have to chop your head off for some reason and apparently you giving me bad news isn't a good enough reason these days! Once I've found him guilty of stealing my tarts, then can I chop off his head?

KING: Why yes of course my love, we just need to seem a bit fairer and kind-

QUEEN: I AM FAIR AND KIND!

KNAVE: Oh no you're not!

QUEEN: Oh yes I am!

KNAVE: Oh no you're not!

QUEEN: Oh yes I am!

KNAVE: Oh no you're not!

QUEEN: Oh yes I am!

KNAVE: Oh no you're not!

QUEEN: Oh shut up! Guards! GUARDS!

(Enter GUARDS)

QUEEN: Take this man away and keep him in the dungeon while he awaits his just and fair trial to be beheaded. You see I'm so kind! Take him away!

TWO OF CLUBS: Right away your Majesty

(The GUARDS exit dragging off the KNAVE OF HEARTS with them)

QUEEN: I'm such a kind person

KING: Yes, you are indeed my love. Jam tart?

> *(The QUEEN opens here mouth, and the KING pushes another jam tart into her mouth.)*

> *(Blackout)*

SCENE TWO

WONDERLAND FOREST

(Enter WALLY)

WALLY: What time is it? *(Audience: you're late!)* Do you know I love living here in Wonderland. There's so many amazing things here in Wonderland! Would you like me to tell you all about them? *(Audience response)*. Well, would you? *(Audience response)* Well, I'm going to anyway!

Song 12 – Twelve Wonders of Wonderland (to the tune of the Twelve Days of Christmas) – DUCHESS, WALLY and ALICE

WALLY: The first wonder of Wonderland my true love gave to me was, A Nice British Cup of Tea

DUCHESS: The second wonder of Wonderland my true love gave to me was, Two Dodos Dancing

ALICE: The third wonder of Wonderland my true love gave to me was, Three drink me potions

WALLY: The fourth wonder of Wonderland my true love gave to me was, Four pocket watches

DUCHESS: The fifth wonder of Wonderland my true love gave to me was, Five Packs of cards

ALICE: The sixth wonder of Wonderland my true love gave to me was, Six giant cupcakes

WALLY: The seventh wonder of Wonderland my true love gave to me was, Seven Tetley tea bags

DUCHESS: The eighth wonder of Wonderland my true love gave to me was, Eight custard tarts

ALICE: The ninth wonder of Wonderland my true love gave to me was, Nine hats from the hatter

WALLY: The tenth wonder of Wonderland my true love gave to me was, Ten dozen roses

DUCHESS: The eleventh wonder of Wonderland my true love gave to me was, Eleven proper poems

ALICE: The twelfth wonder of Wonderland my true love gave to me was, Twelve weeping turtles

(Song finishes)

WALLY: I think we should do that again!

DUCHESS & ALICE: What?!

WALLY: But this time ten times faster!

(The repeat the song one last time but at ten times the speed and starting at twelve this time)

Song 12a – Twelve Wonders of Wonderland (to the tune of the Twelve Days of Christmas) ten times faster – DUCHESS, WALLY and ALICE

(The Song finishes. Exit WALLY, DUCHESS and ALICE. Enter the KNAVE OF HEARTS)

KNAVE: Oh, I wonder where everyone is? Hang on what's that custard pie doing over there? *(Audience: leave the pie alone! Enter DUCHESS followed by WALLY and ALICE.)*

DUCHESS: Who's trying to take my custard pie?

WALLY: What time is it? *(Audience: You're late!)*

DUCHESS: Oh, it's a playing card!

ALICE: I thought it was a guard?

WALLY: It's a playing card guard

DUCHESS: A playing card guard?

ALICE: A card that's a guard and a playing card?

WALLY: Yes, a playing card that's a guard, that's a card!

DUCHESS: Looks like he's a card from a pack, maybe we should put him back in the pack

ALICE: Maybe we should put the card that's a guard and a playing card, back in the pack with the rest of the pack.

WALLY: Well, we'd better make our minds up before this playing card, who's a guard, from a set of cards, who we need to put back in the pack of the playing cards in the pack, before this card from a pack starts to attack.

DUCHESS: I don't think he'll attack, after all he's not actually with a pack, he seems to be separated and perhaps doesn't want to go back to the pack, maybe he's a nice guard, who a playing card, from the back of the pack of playing cards

WALLY: Well I don't think this card, is much of a guard, nor a playing card, so I'd be surprised if he attacked, as he's not with his pack, and it seems he's neither from the back or the front of the pack as there are no other guards nor playing cards with this singular guard, who's a card from a pack of playing cards, who are meant to all be a bunch of playing cards who are also guards, and being as he's on his own, maybe he's on the run at large and if he was going to attack surely he'd have charged, but he's out of breath and not with his pack of cards or as we said any other guards.

KNAVE: Can you say that again?

WALLY: Not a chance!

DUCHESS: But what are you doing here don't you belong at the castle with the Queen of Hearts?

KNAVE: That's where I was, but now I'm on the run as the Queen accused me of stealing her jam tarts! But I've managed to escape. The Queen wanted me to stand trial so she could have me executed.

DUCHESS: So, what was the point of the trial then?

KNAVE: She wanted to come across as fair by giving me a trial.

ALICE: But how can she put you on trial if she's already decided the outcome?

KNAVE: Exactly! Hang on you're Alice, aren't you?

ALICE: Yes, I am. But how do you know who I am?

KNAVE: Everyone in Wonderland knows who you are! You're the girl who fell down the Rabbit hole and is here to save Wonderland from that horrid Queen of Hearts!

ALICE: I don't like the way she rules with an iron fist and how cruel and mean she is to everyone!

WALLY: Yeah so, we've been going round collecting as many people here in Wonderland to stand up to the Queen of Hearts and end her reign of terror once and for all!

DUCHESS: But now we seem to have loads of people on our side, but we haven't really got a plan to stop the Queen at all!

ALICE: Hang on a second, I think I have a plan. Knave of Hearts-

KNAVE: You can call me Jack if you want!

ALICE: Very well Jack, you must go and stand trial.

KNAVE: What?!

ALICE: Trust me no harm will come to you. Once you're standing trial we'll burst into the courtroom and corner the Queen of Hearts-

DUCHESS: Yeah, what then?

ALICE: And I'll tell her to stop being so mean-

DUCHESS: Is that it? You're going to ask her to stop being mean?

ALICE: Yes, I'm going to reason with her.

DUCHESS: You've not met her, have you?

ALICE: No. But I'm sure this will work.

WALLY: It's worth a try… Maybe she'll listen?

ALICE: Don't worry I have a plan B.

DUCHESS: *(Sarcastically)* Oh good because plan A was great.

ALICE: I present to you Plan B. Come on out everyone.

(Suddenly the stage is flooded with characters from Wonderland including; HATTER, DORMOUSE, HARE, CATERPILLAR, CAT, DODO, DUCK, DEE, DUM and several other creatures such as; TURTLE, GRYPHON, several birds etc)

If she doesn't listen to reason that's when all of you lot burst through the doors into the courtroom and demand that the Queen steps down from power. She can't execute all of-

DUCHESS: You really haven't met the Queen, have you?

(People start negatively mumbling 'we might not be able to do it' 'I don't know if this will work etc')

KNAVE: Come on everyone! Alice is right!

Song 13 – Full Company

(At the End of the Song ALICE and the creatures and people of Wonderland stand in strong finishing pose. Blackout)

SCENE THREE

THE QUEENS CASTLE

(Lights up on the QUEEN, KING, FIVE OF CLUBS, ACE OF DIAMONDS, TWO OF HEARTS and EIGHT OF SPADES)

QUEEN: I do love a game of croquet! I always win.

ALL: Yes, your majesty!

QUEEN: Watch this shot! *(The QUEEN takes her first shot. She hits the ball offstage and we hear a loud crash)*

FIVE OF CLUBS: Bad luck your majesty!

QUEEN: What do you mean bad luck? THAT WAS A GREAT SHOT! OFF WITH HIS HEAD! GUARDS! *(Enter GUARDS who drag away FIVE OF CLUBS)*. Well then who's next?

ACE OF DIAMONDS: I'll give it a go! *(ACE OF DIAMONDS takes his shot)*. Wow look at that, what a great shot!

QUEEN: No, it wasn't! You're out. You've lost.

ACE OF DIAMONDS: But-

QUEEN: WHAT DO YOU MEAN BUT? IT WAS A DREADFUL SHOT YOU'RE NOT BETTER THAN ME AT CROQUET! OFF WITH HIS HEAD! GUARDS! GUARDS! OFF WITH HIS HEAD! *(Enter GUARDS who drag away ACE OF DIAMONDS)*. Look at that I'm in first place!

KING: Well done my love you truly are the best!

QUEEN: I know! NEXT PLAYER!

TWO OF HEARTS: I can't seem to find my croquet mallet.

QUEEN: Then that means you can't play, and you lose! OFF WITH HIS HEAD! GUARDS! GUARDS! OFF WITH HIS HEAD! *(Enter GUARDS who drag away TWO OF HEARTS)*. Oh, look I seem to still be in the lead, I really am good at croquet!

KING: You're quite the player my love.

QUEEN: Yes, I am! Tart please! *(The KING pushes a jam tart into the QUEEN'S mouth. Said with a mouthful of jam tart)* NEXT!

EIGHT OF SPADES: Right then here goes.

(EIGHT OF SPADES hits his ball into the wings, we hear

someone shout 'ow!' The stage manager walks on with a bandage on their head looking very annoyed. Exit stage manager)

QUEEN: What a brilliant shot that was well done!

EIGHT OF SPADES: Thank you Mam, may I have a jam tart?

QUEEN: No, they're MINE! OFF WITH HIS HEAD! OFF WITH HIS HEAD! GUARDS! GUARDS! *(Enter GUARDS who drag away EIGHT OF SPADES)*. Oh, look there's no other players left! I win! I win! But I still want to play! BRING ME MY BIGGER RACKET! *(GUARDS enter and hand the QUEEN a Tennis Racket)*

KING: What game shall we play now my love?

QUEEN: I want to play feed the peasants!

KING: And how would one play that my love?

QUEEN: It's easy throw me a jam tart! *(The KING throws a jam tart, and the QUEEN knocks it out into the audience)*

KING: Oh, I like this game! *(The grandstand music plays underneath this scene)*

QUEEN: I know I'm very good at this game I always win! Throw me something else! *(KING throws some cheese balls to the QUEEN which again she knocks out into the audience)* More! More!

KING: How about this? *(KING throws a toilet roll and once again the QUEEN knocks it into the audience)*

QUEEN: More! *(KING throws a tea bag, again the QUEEN knocks it into the audience)* Another!

KING: *(Throws several fairy cakes, counting each one)* 1, 2, 3, 4, 5, 6, 7, 8, 9, 10! Very good my love!

QUEEN: Well, I think that's enough sport for today! I guess that makes me today's winner *(Grandstand theme fades out)*

KING: And such a gracious winner you are!

QUEEN: I know I'm so modest and understated.

Song 14 – QUEEN OF HEARTS

(Blackout)

SCENE FOUR

DUCHESS'S COTTAGE

(Enter WALLY)

WALLY: What time is it? *(Audience: You're late!)*. Where's Mum got too? Hang on what's that custard pie doing over there? *(WALLY move toward the custard pie. Audience: Leave the pie alone!)*

(Enter DUCHESS)

DUCHESS: Who's trying to take my custard pie? Keep your hands off my custard pie! There you are Wally I've been looking for you everywhere!

WALLY: Really?

DUCHESS: Yes. Well, you won't believe it, but I've got me and you a spot at the Wonderland Show Bar!

WALLY: Really? That's amazing? What are we going to do for our act?

DUCHESS: I thought we'd perform our world-famous balloon ballet!

WALLY: But we haven't practised that in years!

DUCHESS: All the more reason to practise now then! Go and get the balloon!

(WALLY exits off to get the balloon and comes back on with the balloon and also wearing a tutu)

Honestly, you're going to love this everyone!

WALLY: Ready!

DUCHESS: You look ridiculous! Honestly a man in a dress, how very silly!

WALLY: Says you!

DUCHESS: Leave it! Right balloon ballet here we go then! Music please *(Ballet music plays)*

(WALLY and DUCHESS perform the balloon ballet. First, they roll the balloon between both of their hands without dropping it. However, the DUCHESS manages to get whacked on the hand)

DUCHESS: Ouch my hand *(rubbing her hand)*.

WALLY: Are you alright Mum?

DUCHESS: It's okay I'll get *(name of the man she picked on at the start)* to kiss it better! *(goes to the man she picked on at the start and gets him to kiss it better)* That's much better! Thank you *(insert name here)*. Now we'll do it again but this time you go through my legs!

WALLY: What? *(WALLY accidentally hits DUCHESS in the face whilst exclaiming 'what?')*

DUCHESS: Oh, you've hit me right on my cheek! *(Rubbing her face)*

WALLY: Are you alright Mum?

DUCHESS: It's okay I'll get *(name of the man she picked on at the start)* to kiss it better again! *(goes to the man she picked on at the start and gets him to kiss it better)* That's much better! Thank you *(insert name here)*. Now let's try this again shall we Wally! *(DUCHESS places the balloon between herself and WALLY. The balloon is now both on WALLY and DUCHESS'S chests)* And music! *(Ballet music plays)*

(WALLY goes through DUCHESS'S legs whilst keeping the balloon between them without dropping it)

DUCHESS: Right now, back the other way!

WALLY: What?

DUCHESS: Come back through! Music! *(Ballet music plays. On the last attempt when they go backwards the balloon pops on the DUCHESS'S bottom)* Oh that popped right on my bottom *(rubbing her bottom)*

WALLY: Are you alright Mum?

DUCHESS: *(Turns and looks straight at the man she picked on at the start of the show again)* No! I think *(insert name here)* will have to kiss it better! *(Duchess starts to make her way down the stairs to the audience)*

WALLY: *(Gets out his pocket watch)* Hang on Mum! We're late!

DUCHESS: Oh no! I'm so sorry *(insert name here)* you'll have to come and kiss it better after the show, dressing room one!

WALLY: Come on Mum let's go!

(Ballet music plays them off. Exit DUCHESS and WALLY)

(Blackout)

SCENE FIVE

THE QUEENS CASTLE

(The lights come up on a courtroom setting. The judge is the KING OF HEARTS, who has the QUEEN sat next to him and the jury is packed with all different card guards and the KNAVE OF HEARTS is standing trial. Everyone is talking)

KING: *(Bangs his gavel)* Order, order *(Everyone is still talking)* Order, order!

QUEEN: Everybody SHUT UP!

KING: Thank you my love. We are here today for the trail of the Knave of Hearts, who has been accused-

QUEEN: And is guilty! OFF WITH HIS HEAD!

KING: Not yet my love, jam tart?

QUEEN: Yes please *(opens her mouth and the KING pushes in a jam tart)*

KING: Knave of Hearts you have been accused of stealing the Queens Jam tarts

(Jury all begin to murmur and chat)

KING: *(Bangs his gavel)* Order, order *(Everyone is still talking)* Order, order!

QUEEN: Everybody listen! Jam tart please!

KING: Here you are my love *(places another jam tart into the QUEEN'S mouth)*. Knave you are here today to plead your case! How is it you plead

KNAVE: Not guilty

JURY: *(GASP)*

QUEEN: Liar!

KING: *(Shoves another jam tart in the QUEEN'S mouth)* Now it has been said that you stole a jam tart, why should I the judge and they the jury believe you? What is it that makes you innocent?

KNAVE: I'm allergic to jam!

JURY: *(GASP and begin talking again)*

KING: *(Bangs his gavel)* Order, order *(Everyone is still talking)* Order, order!

QUEEN: EVERYBODY BE QUIET! WE'RE TRYING TO HAVE A FAIR TRIAL SO I CAN CHOP OFF HIS HEAD!

KING: *(Shoves another jam tart into the QUEEN'S mouth)* I don't believe you when you say you're allergic to jam!

KNAVE: But it's the truth!

KING: Oh no it isn't!

KNAVE: Oh yes it is!

KING: Oh no it isn't!

KNAVE: Oh yes it is!

KING: Oh no it isn't!

KNAVE: Oh yes it is!

KING: It seems that the common people seem to believe you-

QUEEN: WELL, I DON'T! OFF WITH HIS HEAD *(Again the KING puts another jam tart in the QUEEN'S mouth)*

KING: I would say that you are nothing more than a liar and a sinner! And I don't believe your story and neither do the jury. So I have no choice but to sentence you-

KNAVE: Wait, wait! Before you sentence me let me tell you a story that may perhaps change your mind! It's about a dream I had!

Song 15 – KNAVE and JURY

(Song ends with KNAVE and the JURY in end poses)

KING: Guilty! *(Bangs his gavel)*

QUEEN: OFF WITH HIS HEAD! OFF WITH HIS HEAD! GUARDS! GUARDS!

(ALICE bursts into the court room)

ALICE: Not so fast!

JURY: *(GASP)*

QUEEN: You must be the girl who fell down the rabbit hole!

ALICE: That's me and I've come to ask you if you'll consider being a nicer person

QUEEN: Let me think about it *(pauses for a brief moment)*. I've thought about it. No. OFF WITH HER HEAD! OFF WITH HER HEAD!

ALICE: I was hoping you weren't going to say that *(ALICE whistles and WALLY, HATTER, HARE, DORMOUSE, CATERPILLAR, CAT, DODO, DUCK, DEE, DUM and various other creatures from Wonderland enter)*

WALLY: What time is it? *(Audience: You're late!)*

QUEEN: What is the meaning of all this!

HARE: We're fed up with you ruling over Wonderland with an iron fist!

WALLY: Yeah, you're making our lives a misery!

DORMOUSE: And we're here to make you step down from power!

QUEEN: I'll never step aside Wonderland is mine! IT'S ALL MINE, MINE, MINE, MINE! GUARDS! GUARDS!

(Enter GUARDS)

Take all of these traitors away immediately and OFF WITH ALL OF THEIR HEADS!

(Enter DUCHESS with a leaf blower)

DUCHESS: Hey! You stupid pack of cards, have some of this! *(Turns on the leaf blower and blows away all of the guards)*

ALICE: Now your guards are gone and you're powerless!

QUEEN: What? But- My King what can we do?

KING: I don't know! I think the games up! *(Runs off screaming)*

QUEEN: Come back you coward! Fine I'll face you myself you stupid girl! *(QUEEN draws her sword)*

ALICE: If it's a fight you want, then you've got it! *(CAT throws ALICE a sword)*

(ALICE and the QUEEN have a sword fight and ALICE ends up victorious, knocking the QUEEN to the floor)

QUEEN: Okay, okay! I give up! I give up!

ALICE: Now hand over your crown!

QUEEN: Here take it! Take it just please have mercy!

ALICE: We will now have a new Queen of Wonderland. Duchess Dolly step forward.

DUCHESS: Me a Queen?

WALLY: I thought you already were?

DUCHESS: What?

WALLY: Never mind!

ALICE: All Hail Queen Dolly Dollop of Wonderland!

ALL: *(Cheer)*

CAT: Hey baby look at that it's a happy ending here in Wonderland!

HATTER: What a mad day it's been!

DORMOUSE: What should we do with the now former Queen?

WALLY: *(To the audience)* What do you think we should do with her boys and girls? *(audience response)* There's a kid at the back shouting kill her-

DUCHESS: Must be from *(local reference)*. I've got an idea I can finally put my custard pie to good use! *(Goes over and gets the custard pie)* Now then boys and girls, shall I let the former Queen, have it? *(Audience response)*. Shall I give the former Queen a custard pie? *(Audience response)*. Very well then! *(DUCHESS pushes the pie into the QUEEN'S face)*

ALL: *(Cheer)*

ALICE: *(To the QUEEN)* You are now banished from Wonderland! And you will live out the rest of your days in a far-off desolate and miserable land!

QUEEN: Please have mercy!

ALICE: You will spend the rest of your days in *(local reference)*!

QUEEN: No please anything but that! *(Runs off)*

WALLY: Well would you look at that a happy ending!

HATTER: Though it does feel like there's something missing!

DORMOUSE: Yes, don't we normally have a wedding at the end of these things?

KNAVE: Stand aside everyone! Queen Dolly, it would be my honour if I could sit beside you as your King and rule Wonderland with you, you have stolen my heart. Will you marry me?

DUCHESS: Of yes of course I will!

KNAVE: You truly are the most beautiful woman in the world!

WALLY: Not seen that many women then?

DUCHESS: I'm getting married and Wonderland is safe! And it's all thanks to Alice.

WALLY: Three cheers for Alice everyone! Hip hip!

ALL: Hooray!

WALLY: Hip hip!

ALL: Hooray!

WALLY: Hip hip!

ALL: Hooray!

Song 16 – All (Apart from KING & QUEEN)

(At the end of the song WALLY steps forward as the curtains close)

SCENE SIX

IN FRONT OF TABS

WALLY: What time is it? *(Audience: You're late!)*. Did you all enjoy the show? *(Audience response)* Can you believe it a happy ending! Wonderland is safe and sound and Mum's the new Queen, which I guess makes me a Prince and she's getting married as well! Now I have got a few shout-outs to do, so without further ado *(insert shouts and birthday announcements etc here)* Do you know what I'm so happy I could sing a song and just so happens I've got a song we can all join in with! I'll sing it first and then you can join in afterwards.

Song 17 – Songsheet – WALLY

(Enter DUCHESS)

DUCHESS: Did I hear some singing?

WALLY: You did indeed Mum! Would you like to join in with everyone else this time?

DUCHESS: Would I ever!

WALLY: Music please!

Song 17a – Songsheet – WALLY & DUCHESS

DUCHESS: Do you know what Wally I think this side of the room, let's just call them my side, were much louder than the other side of the room let's just call them your side!

WALLY: That sounds like fighting talking to me!

DUCHESS: Don't talk about fighting the lot from *(local reference)* at the back might get the wrong idea!

WALLY: Well, what about my side versus your side?

DUCHESS: You're on. You can go first!

WALLY: Very well come on my side up on your feet! Here we go!

Song 17b – Songsheet – WALLY

DUCHESS: What a load of rubbish! Come on my side up you get! Let's show them how it's done! Music please!

Song 17c – Songsheet – DUCHESS

DUCHESS: Well, I think it's safe to say my side, was the winning side!

WALLY: Hang on, you can't just say your side was the winning side!

DUCHESS: But they were-

WALLY: Look, we'll have to get an independent judge.

(Enter HATTER)

HATTER: I'll be the judge!

WALLY: Brilliant in that case we'll both sing it one more time. Then you can decide, which side are the winners!

HATTER: Sounds like a great idea to me!

DUCHESS: Very well then everybody let's do it one more time! Music please!

Song 17d – Songsheet – WALLY & DUCHESS

HATTER: I have come to my decision and the winning side is… Can I get a drum roll please! This side *(points to the winning side. DUCHESS and WALLY react to the winning side)*. Right, I'm off see you all later everyone!

DUCHESS: I've got to be going as well as I've got a wedding to get ready for! See you later everyone!

WALLY: Well, I suppose we better sing it altogether one last time before I go!

Song 17e – Songsheet – WALLY

WALLY: What time is it? *(Audience: you're late!)* See you later everyone!

(Exit WALLY)

BOWS

ALICE: We hope you enjoyed your trip to Wonderland.

DUCHESS: I'm now married, regal, royal and grand

HATTER: I'm still a Hatter mad as can be

QUEEN: I'm stuck in *(local reference)* there's not much to see

WALLY: I'm running late and still not on time

KNAVE: Me and my new Queen will be just fine

DEE & DUM: We've had such fun with you all

CAT: I'm still a grinning Cat, and I'm cool

DORMOUSE: So, whether you've come from far or near

ALL: We hope to see you all next year!

    Song 18 – Finale – All

    (END)

Also by Joe Meloy and available from Beercott Books

Beauty and the BEAST

Set in the quaint little French village of [INSERT LOCAL REFERENCE HERE!], not far from [ANOTHER LOCAL REFERENCE!] is where our tale is set. Will the Beast be able to find true love before it's too late, will our dastardly villain Lucas Luxuriant get his comeuppance? Will Fairy Dust help save the day, and will Potty Pierre and Madame Marie Macaroon be able to get dinner ready and keep the Beast from going feral? Find out in this Pantomime adventure packed with fantastic gags, slapstick and something for all the family!

SNOW WHITE And the Seven Dwarfs

Will our dashing Prince save the day? Will Dame Maisy Marmalade and Muddles be more of a help than hindrance? Are the Dwarfs actually Dwarfs? And will the #Selfie obsessed Evil Queen be stopped? Join us in the Pantomime story of Snow White & the Seven Dwarfs!

Packed out with hilarious comedy routines and of course plenty of audience participation this Panto will have the whole family laughing and asking for more! OH YES IT WILL!

About the author

I'm Joe Meloy ('...the excellent pantomime dame...' British Theatre Guide) and I'm an Actor, Pantomime Dame, Producer and Panto Enthusiast. I attended my first Pantomime when I was three and instantly fell in love with one of the most entertaining forms of theatre, in my humble opinion of course!

I have been performing in pantomime myself for a number of years having played Widow Twankey to an Ugly Sister, there have been one or two occasions where I haven't been in the dress, but I much prefer putting on my dresses, fake eyelashes and lip stick!

I performed my first professional Pantomime at twenty-three years old playing an Ugly Sister in an adult pantomime. I returned the next year to perform as Widow Twankey, from there I went on to play in family pantomimes as; Widow Twankey (twice more!) Dame Dolly Dollop, Nurse Nellie, King Arthur and as Maid Joan for the Hazlitt Theatre.